Original title:
Ivy Interludes

Author: Elliot Harrison
ISBN HARDBACK: 978-1-80566-735-3
ISBN PAPERBACK: 978-1-80566-864-0

Echoes of Verdant Dreams

In the garden, plants conspire,
Whispers of joy, they never tire.
A snail sporting a tiny hat,
Waddles by a chubby cat.

Laughter ripples through the leaves,
As butterflies wear festive sleeves.
The sun winks at the daffodils,
While frogs practice acrobatics on hills.

A Dance of Tendrils and Time

Tendrils twirl like ribbons spun,
Dancing under the playful sun.
A beetle leads the merry sway,
While daisies cheer, hip hip hooray!

The gnomes giggle in their hats,
As squirrels try on fancy spats.
Each petal flutters with delight,
In this whimsical green-fingered fight.

Lattice of Nature's Secrets

In the vines, secrets spill,
Like gossiping winds that trill.
A turtle with a wise insight,
Sips tea while the day turns bright.

Each leaf dons a tiptoe smile,
As bees buzz about with style.
The trees chuckle, old and stout,
In a grand leafy shout-out.

The Silent Gaze of the Green

The leaves play peek-a-boo with light,
Each shadow dances, a playful sight.
A rabbit dons a detective’s guise,
Searching for his missing fries!

With every breeze, they share a lark,
The mushrooms giggle in the dark.
A garden full of jests and glee,
Nature's laughter, wild and free.

The Gravity of Climbing Green

A vine once tried to touch the sky,
But slipped on dew, oh my, oh my!
It tangled up a curious bee,
Who buzzed, "This isn’t meant for me!"

Leaves laughed as they danced in the breeze,
While critters waved with such ease.
Each branch took on a playful role,
As giggles rolled and took their toll.

In Nature’s Humble Grasp

A squirrel claimed his throne with flair,
On roots that twisted everywhere.
He wore a crown of grass and twine,
Exclaiming, "Nature, all is mine!"

A rabbit joined, with a swift hop,
Claiming shortcuts, zooming nonstop.
They laughed and pranced with jovial cheer,
While flowers clapped, “Come join us here!”

The Secret Life of Climbing Hearts

A lizard dreamed of rock-star fame,
With headphones on, he played a game.
He slipped and slid, a graceful fall,
“Next time I'll stick it!” was his call.

Flowers whispered secrets sweet,
To bees who danced on tiny feet.
While petals plotted discreet schemes,
Creating chaos in their dreams.

Soft Shadows on Stony Paths

The stones lay snoozing, what a sight,
As shadows stretched in soft moonlight.
A hedgehog snoffed, then rolled about,
With twigs as swords, he waved, no doubt!

While crickets chirped a merry tune,
Underneath the watchful moon.
With every step upon the way,
Laughter echoed, brightened the day.

Veins of a Forgotten Wall

Once a wall, so proud and tall,
Now trapped by leaves that slyly sprawl.
A garden gnome just rolls his eyes,
As nature's quirk catches surprise.

With every twist and every turn,
The vines explore, they laugh and churn.
A lizard grins, a squirrel sighs,
They hold a contest, who's more wise?

The bricks beneath their leafy dress,
Whisper tales of wild excess.
Adventurous sprouts, they claim the crown,
While local bugs dance upside down.

Who knew a wall could spark such fun,
With leafy champs and rays of sun?
A merry jest, a timeless thrall,
Life's a party on a forgotten wall.

Echoes Beneath the Canopy

Under leaves where shadows play,
Mischief-makers come out to sway.
1-2-3 and off they go,
To cause a ruckus in the show.

Squirrels chatter, birds dive low,
A playful breeze puts on a show.
Tickle the flowers, bop the trees,
Nature's laughter floats on the breeze.

The tall grass whispers jokes of old,
To every creature, brave and bold.
A tongue-tied snail, a winking bee,
Join in the chorus, wild and free.

Underneath, the roots will giggle,
At every sprout's ridiculous wiggle.
Their leafy secrets shared in jest,
Beneath the canopy, we've been blessed.

Secrets of the Climbing Vine

Oh, the secrets that they keep,
Those climbing vines that twist and creep.
With every knot and tangled spin,
They plot and scheme amid the din.

A curious cat surveys the scene,
While buzzing bugs buzz in between.
They giggle, tickling leaves galore,
As vine wraps round an old oak door.

Mice convene with whispers sly,
Trading tales while the moon swings high.
A flower blushing from the tease,
Yearns for the day, the vines, the breeze.

Secrets hidden, laughter flows,
Under arches where no one goes.
What mischief waits, what games divine,
In the world of the climbing vine.

Tangles of Time and Nature

Tangles weave through histories grand,
A jester's play in a green wonderland.
Round and round, both fast and slow,
Nature laughs at her secret show.

With wobbly roots and branches slim,
Even the bravest might feel grim.
But giggles echo through the air,
As creatures dance without a care.

An ancient tree with gnarled frown,
Holds tales of mischief all around.
Its knots are friends to those who dare,
To share a laugh, a secret prayer.

Through tangled days, we find our rhyme,
In the joyful games of silly time.
Oh, what a laughter, nature's call,
In the tangled dance where we stand tall.

The Poetry Between Vines

In a garden where laughter sings,
Twists and turns like elastic strings.
Leaves whisper secrets, oh what a jest,
Nature's jokes, we love them best.

Dancing leaves with a playful sway,
Nature holds its bright ballet.
Buds giggle as they bloom and stretch,
A vine's wild antics, hard to sketch.

Beneath the sun, they chat and tease,
Winding around with charming ease.
A serpent of green with a wink and grin,
Here’s to the glee that vines begin.

The Freedom of Intertwining Roots

Beneath the soil, a party brews,
Roots high-fiving, sharing news.
With each twist, they share a laugh,
Tangled together, it's quite the craft.

Subterranean shenanigans abound,
Each loop and curl making merry sound.
Dancing in dirt like a silly troupe,
Roots break barriers, join the group.

With a wink, they stretch and play,
Finding adventures in the clay.
Intertwining tales, no need for far,
Together they shine, like twinkling stars.

A Reverie of Climbing Beauty

Up the wall, a bold ascent,
Climbing with style, a vine's own event.
A daring leap, then a graceful crawl,
No hesitation, just stand tall!

With every reach, a chuckle grows,
As if the sky were in on the show.
Detouring past clouds, they glint with mirth,
A climb of laughter here on earth.

Tendrils reach with a whimsy charm,
They're plotting high, but won't do harm.
In this playful race, the sun their friend,
They climb for joy, from start to end.

Dreams Cradled in Green

In the blanket of leaves, dreams reside,
Where giggles echo, and humor hides.
A cozy nook where thoughts entwine,
With a flourish of green, all's divine.

Whispers of vines, secrets to share,
Where wishes climb high in the sunny air.
Wrapped in foliage, cozy and sweet,
Life’s little quirks, a charming treat.

Nestled in nature’s playful hand,
A sanctuary built, oh so grand.
With every green hug, laughter springs,
In dreams embraced, the joy it brings.

Flourish in the Sheltering Green

In the garden, a gnome does dance,
With a hat so tall, it twirls at a glance.
Plants whisper secrets, they giggle and sigh,
While bees buzz around, they aim for the pie.

Mushrooms wear spots like a lady's dress,
But watch out, my friend, they cause quite the mess!
Frogs leap in boots made of big, squishy moss,
And rabbits, in bow ties, just can't help but floss.

Echoes of Life's Climbing Story

A snail in a tie crawls up the fence,
He plots out a course, oh so very intense.
“Slow and steady,” he says with a grin,
While squirrels laugh loud, “We’ll never let you win!”

Ladders made of twigs lay scattered 'round,
As critters embark on journeys unbound.
A raccoon recites a poem about cheese,
While laughing hyenas swing from the trees.

Whispers of Green Tendrils

Tendrils that tickle and twist with delight,
Hold on to the rooftops, scaling the height.
“Watch me climb,” cries the proud little vine,
“Next stop, the top! I’ll feel so divine!”

A squirrel named Chip borrowed a chair,
To oversee all the critters' fair share.
Do frogs wear pajamas? The answer's a shout:
“Only on weekends!” they croak, then they pout.

The Lattice of Life

In a trellis of tales where secrets collide,
The creatures of fun all gather with pride.
A hedgehog with sunglasses chuckles at flies,
While a turtle in goggles contemplates the skies.

The daisies debate who's the brightest of all,
As the sun gives a wink, oh so grand and tall.
Caterpillars swing as they plot their next moves,
While ants pull a prank in their tiny old grooves.

The Elysian Tangle

In gardens where the mischief thrives,
A twist of green that truly strives.
Each leaf a grin, each tendril plays,
In silent pranks, the sunshine stays.

A fellow plant with lofty dreams,
Wants to climb, or so it seems.
But tangled up, it trips and falls,
While laughing leaves parade their brawls.

The pollen dances, bees come near,
Making jokes we cannot hear.
Among the roots, the laughter grows,
As vines engage in friendly throes.

And when the sun begins to fade,
They swap their stories, homemade aid.
With every twist, a punchline's charm,
In this green laughter, who means harm?

Beneath the Leafy Embrace

Beneath the canopy so thick,
Lies lovely laughter, quick and slick.
Frogs croak jokes to the buzzing bees,
As squirrels plan their nutty keys.

A chubby snail steals a ray of sun,
While grasshoppers dance just for fun.
The shadows join in, unaware,
They trip on roots — oh, what a scare!

The dandelions spin tall tales,
Of lofty dreams caught in the gales.
A wise old oak rolls its wise eyes,
While buzzing flies share clever lies.

In this embrace of leafy cheer,
Every creature has its peer.
With giggles echoing ‘round the bend,
It’s a garden party without end!

The Journey Upwards

A sprout with hope, it stretches high,
Past all the bugs that pass it by.
With every inch, it tells a joke,
To cheer the ants, all in a cloak.

The sunbeams laugh, a golden team,
While raindrops wink, a crafty scheme.
But oh! A gust sends it askew,
It does a spin – now what to do?

Branches wave, 'Just dance and sway!'
As the little sprout finds its way.
Its leaves like hands, they clap and cheer,
Who knew that growth could bring such cheer?

So up it goes, with every leap,
Through blustery winds, its secrets keep.
A rootsy cheer for all the vines,
In comedy, nature often shines!

Whispers Among the Climbing Vines

Among the twists, the whispers flow,
As vines begin their lively show.
They tickle walls and tease the sky,
While critters pause to wonder why.

Each tendril tells a different tale,
Of daring dreams, they shall not fail.
A squirrel giggles at their fight,
While butterflies dance in pure delight.

The climbing game ignites the jest,
With wriggling roots, they'd surely best.
Laughter echoes in leafy gloom,
Creating joy in every room.

The sun looks down, it can't resist,
A chuckle joins the leafy twist.
For in this tangle, life's a jest,
Nature's theater, simply the best!

Tales of Time in Emerald Cloak

Under green drapes, the squirrels convene,
Telling jokes about a tree that's obscene.
A butterfly sneezes, the branches all shake,
Laughter erupts with each giggle and quake.

The owls hoot loudly, in fits of delight,
While the frogs sing ballads deep into the night.
A raccoon wears glasses, pretending he's wise,
With a map in his paws, oh, what a surprise!

In the daytime, the shadows write rhymes,
As the sun sets, they commit silly crimes.
A dance on the leaves, they twirl and they spin,
With mirth in the air, everyone joins in.

Time's a jester, in this leafy domain,
With chuckles and giggles, it twists like a chain.
Each moment a gem in the emerald haze,
In tales of laughter, forever we gaze.

Beneath Arching Canopies

Beneath the branches, the shadows collide,
A parade of critters, oh what a ride!
A gopher in tutu, a badger in shoes,
Dance past a snail who's refusing to lose.

The leaves whisper secrets of frivolous feats,
While the ants throw a party with crumbs for treats.
A turtle plays cards with a wise old crow,
But ignores the rules, oh how low can you go!

A chipmunk recites silly limericks loud,
While the fireflies twinkle, all dressed like a crowd.
From every branch, giggles flutter like leaves,
Creating a symphony only joy weaves.

As twilight descends, the rabble grows bold,
With songs of the silly, and tales retold.
In the fun of the night, friendships ignite,
Beneath arching canopies, all feels just right.

Enigmas of the Verdant Veil

In the canopy thick, where shadows do dance,
A lizard plays charades, oh what a chance!
His moves are the talk of the leafy brigade,
As laughter erupts in a colorful parade.

A cunning old fox juggles acorns with flair,
While the rabbits all cheer, with carrots to share.
A tortoise complains it's all just too fast,
Yet joins in the mirth, the fun unsurpassed!

With giggles that ripple through every thick leaf,
The whispers of woodland mix joy with some grief.
For who knew that fun could orchestrate dreams,
In a world made of laughter and silly schemes?

As dusk weaves its cloak, the jokes only grow,
In the verdant veil where the antics flow.
Each riddle unraveled, each giggle a cheer,
In the realm of the wild, there's nothing to fear.

The Essence of the Vined Hours

In tangled embrace, the vines twist and sway,
While chameleons chuckle, just basking in play.
A quizzical lizard dons bright polka dots,
And claims to be fashion's most edgy in plots.

The wise old tortoise spins tales of the past,
While the grasshoppers leap, filling up fast.
With leaps and a bounce, they all gather round,
For stories of mischief in laughter abound.

The moments unfold, like a never-ending reel,
As smiles entwine with the joy that we feel.
A raccoon steals snacks from beneath the great vine,
But the laughter erupts, oh the fun’s divine!

With each little hour, the jokes intertwine,
As whimsy grows wild with the dawn's silken shine.
For in the vined hours, there’s always a jest,
In a world made of chuckles, we feel truly blessed.

The Veil of Nature’s Whispers

In the garden, vines entwine,
Chasing squirrels, feeling fine.
They laugh and leap upon the wall,
Nature's jesters, having a ball.

Beneath the leaves, a riddle grows,
Where do the chubby gnomes go?
Hiding from the playful breeze,
Wearing hats that dance with ease.

Lively birds prance with delight,
Stealing snacks from ants at night.
One slips, tumbles, makes a fuss,
In the chaos, nature’s plus.

With every rustle, giggles sound,
The flora’s laughter knows no bound.
In this circus of the green,
Every leaf’s a dance routine.

Tales of Nature's Embrace

A crooked tree wears glasses wide,
Admiring bugs that glide and slide.
“Look at me! I’m quite the sight!”
Said a ladybug, color bright.

The bumblebee with fuzzy hair,
Sings opera in the fragrant air.
The flowers join, a chorus loud,
Making nature feel so proud.

A snail slips by, takes its sweet time,
Dreaming of a day to climb.
“Catch me if you can!” it shouts,
While the rush of life pouts and scouts.

Dandelions toss their heads,
While rabbits weave between their beds.
In this playground, day by day,
Nature’s humor comes to play.

Nature’s Tender Language

Whispers of leaves dance in the breeze,
Squirrels giggle up high in the trees.
Flowers gossip, oh what a tease,
While bees buzz round with such great ease.

A snail tells tales of days gone by,
Laughing with grasshoppers, oh my, oh my!
The robin sings, a raspy reply,
While ants parade under the blue sky.

The Play of Light and Leaf

Sunbeams dappling through the green,
Make shadows dance, a quirky scene.
A leaf on the ground, it thinks it’s keen,
But a gust of wind says, "Not your routine!"

The branches wave, a jester's hat,
While squirrels plot to sneak by the cat.
Nature's laughter, can you hear that?
Even the mushrooms join in the spat!

A Story Suspended in Time

In the quiet glade where stories hide,
An acorn dreams of its future wide.
A wise old tree sways with pride,
While frogs make bets on the river side.

A picnic of ants in their grand parade,
Tell tales of the crumbs that they have made.
While a butterfly flirts, so unafraid,
With a petal, on fun they'll trade!

The Grace of an Ascending Nature

A vine climbs up, a curious quest,
With sticky fingers, it takes a rest.
The flowers cheer, they're feeling blessed,
While the sun grins down, it knows best.

A worm in the soil, a comedian's role,
Telling the roots they're on a stroll.
The moonlight twinkles, a wink of a soul,
In nature's realm, laughter's the goal!

Melodies of the Untamed Wall

A wall so wild, it sings a tune,
With plants that dance beneath the moon.
They tickle bricks in cheerful glee,
Oh, what a sight, it's quite the spree!

A lizard leaps, a squirrel twirls,
With leafy friends, they share their pearls.
The flowers nod, as if to say,
"Join in the fun, don't shy away!"

In every crack and every space,
A melody finds its happy place.
Who knew a garden could entertain,
With laughter sprouting like sweet champagne?

So come and hear the stories told,
In tales of green that never grow old.
Under the sun, we laugh and play,
As nature's band leads us astray!

Reflections in a Greener Veil

A mirror made of leaves so bright,
Shows giggles hiding in plain sight.
Each vine a story, each leaf a laugh,
Nature's fool, a whimsical gaffe!

Toads wear crowns of dewy gold,
While bumblebees are brave and bold.
With every hop and every buzz,
They orchestrate a joyful fuzz!

Puddles shimmer with each sweet glance,
As flowers prance in a silly dance.
Reflecting smiles from roots to skies,
Who knew being green could be so wise?

So take a peek in nature's ride,
Where humor blooms and joy won't hide.
In leafy realms, the laughter swells,
With echoes of mirth from those green wells!

The Tender Touch of Nature's Grip

A hand of green reaches out to play,
With leafy fingers that sway all day.
They tickle toes as they scurry near,
Whispering secrets for all to hear!

The daisies giggle, the roses wink,
In a world where madness makes you think.
Nature’s grip is a warm embrace,
Inviting all to share the space!

The wind joins in for a jolly spree,
Tickling trunks of the tallest tree.
Every branch a joke that's falling down,
Nature's humor wears the crown!

So let us twirl with the leaves so spry,
With laughter echoing 'neath the sky.
In nature's grip, we find our grace,
A comical dance in this splendid place!

Embraced by the Thorned Whispers

Thorns of laughter prick the air,
In a garden where jokes dare to share.
With every brush of nature's tease,
Comes a chuckle from rustling leaves!

The brambles giggle, poking fun,
At the clumsy bumblebees on the run.
"Watch your step!" they seem to call,
As petals flutter, standing tall!

In tangled vines, a riddle grows,
Where witticisms tumble like prose.
Each thorn a pun, sharp and sweet,
In this lush chaos, we find our beat!

So join the jests, embrace the sting,
Where nature’s humor reigns as king.
In whispers green, we dance and sway,
In thorny laughter, we find our way!

Whispers in the Woven Vines

In a garden where mischief brews,
Laughter echoes with playful cues.
A sneaky vine from right to left,
It tickles toes, oh what a theft!

The flowers giggle, dance in glee,
Telling secrets, 'Come see, come see!'
A gourd from above falls right on cue,
In the tangle, friendship blooms anew.

From twirling leaves, a message flies,
‘Pick me up, I’m full of lies!’
A squirrel steals a snack with flair,
While vines share whispers in the air.

Each twist and turn a clever joke,
Unruly greens beneath the oak.
With laughter spilling from the ground,
In leafy laughter, joy is found.

Beneath the Canopy of Green

Underneath a leafy dome,
Critters gather, feeling home.
A rabbit wears a funny hat,
While the birds chirp, 'Imagine that!'

Mice in sneakers race through trails,
On tiny bikes with tiny sails.
While ants conduct a marching band,
With a rhythm they truly planned!

A bushy tail sways to the beat,
As frogs croak along, tapping their feet.
With a kingdom of giggles in the shade,
The best of fun is grandly displayed.

Beneath this green, the world's a jest,
Where nature's creatures have the best fest.
With laughter rising up so clear,
In playful glee, we hold so dear.

The Language of Climbing Shadows

Shadows dance on the garden wall,
Making faces, oh what a brawl!
With each twist, they prance and glide,
Giving clues of what they hide.

An impostor vine with a cheeky grin,
A patch of leaves claims, 'I’m the kingpin!'
Nearby, a squirrel makes quite the scene,
As shadows chatter, it’s all routine.

In this realm where laughter grows,
Each shadow speaks in silly prose.
'Climb aboard!' the whisper calls,
Where humor rises and never falls.

The antics weave a playful show,
Each leaf a partner in this flow.
Through giggles shared in leafy shade,
The language of fun is finely displayed.

Secrets in the Leafy Embrace

In the nook where secrets hide,
A raccoon winks and takes a ride.
Tangles of greens, a fortress grand,
With herbs that laugh at a busy hand.

The chattering brook joins in the song,
'Come laugh with us where you belong!'
A snail in sneakers takes its time,
While shadows giggle, keeping rhyme.

Butterflies play peek-a-boo,
In the leafy hug that feels so true.
A garden gnome with a silly hat,
Shares jokes with the frogs, imagine that!

Within these greens, we share a grin,
With every flutter, let's begin.
In the embrace of joy so sweet,
Life blooms wildly, never discreet.

A Tapestry of Green and Gold

In a garden where laughter blooms,
Tangles of green wear silly costumes.
Frogs jump madly, croak a tune,
While snails play tag beneath the moon.

Leaves dance lightly in morning’s glow,
Whispers of glee where wild grass grows.
A hedgehog pirouettes with flair,
While daisies gossip without a care.

Visions from the Emerald Ascent

Climbing high on a wobbly vine,
Squirrels shout jokes over chilled wine.
The branches creak, a comedy show,
As ants debate who stole the crow.

Buds of laughter pop open wide,
As chubby bunnies host a slide.
A colorful lizard with shades of blue,
Keeps time with a wiggle and a little moo.

The Heartbeat of the Climbing Art

In the treetops, mischief brews,
Parrots play tricks on sleepy snooze.
A raccoon juggles acorns with glee,
While monkeys swing—a lively spree!

At sunset, the vines throw a fête,
Glowing lights, oh, what a state!
The moon's the DJ, spinning tunes,
While fireflies dance in bright costumes.

Verdant Chronicles of the Hidden

Under leaves where secrets lie,
Mice write tales of a butterfly.
A turtle dreams of becoming spry,
While dragonflies explore the sky.

From shadows emerge a playful crowd,
Frolicking creatures oh-so-proud.
They plot and scheme, but all in jest,
In their world, every day’s a fest!

A Tapestry of Flourishing Love

In the garden, laughter blooms,
Twisting tales among the looms.
Petals dance on whims anew,
Love's a stain that won't undo.

Strange things grow from tiny seeds,
Whispering of romance needs.
A vine creeps up to steal a kiss,
With roots that find pure comedy bliss.

Colors clash in wild embrace,
Nature plays a painted face.
The sun laughs at the moonlight flee,
Together they make quite the spree.

A tapestry of blooper vines,
Unraveling through hearty signs.
Each giggle woven in the thread,
A funny love, both green and red.

Flourish and Fade

Green tongues wiggle in the breeze,
Tickling noses of the bees.
With every twist and twirl so bright,
We laugh at things that take to flight.

Fleeting blooms, they shed their grace,
While we dance and make our case.
Roots are tangled like our jokes,
Flourish and fade, among the folks.

Shadows play on sunlit paths,
Nature smiles, it loves to laugh.
Two leaves chase, a game of tag,
While in the back, a snail’s a brag.

Time giggles at what it parades,
Seeing life in quick cascades.
Even weeds have funny roots,
Growing tales of wild pursuits.

The Language of Clarity

In whispers green beneath the sky,
Laughter rises as leaves fly.
A syllable of rustling cheer,
Nature sings, it’s crystal clear.

Words grow wild among the vines,
Jokes are made on twisting lines.
They tickle hearts, so carefree,
A giggle shared, a tapestry.

The critters join this comic sound,
In every branch, a jest is found.
Let’s translate all this leafy fun,
As sunshine tries to out-run the run.

Amid the greens, a freedom soars,
Finding joy in what it pours.
In this language, laugh and play,
Nature’s whimsy leads the way.

Green Against the Mortar

Between the cracks, the laughter grows,
A sprout pokes through, and all it knows.
It stretches forth, a cheeky grin,
Defying walls that hide its skin.

Gentle jests like petals rain,
Tickling bricks with sprightly gain.
Each leaf a quip, its sprightly tone,
A comedy in stone alone.

The mortar cracks, it starts to sing,
Nature's voice in playful fling.
The bricks may frown, but can't despair,
For greens will thrive with lively flair.

What's strong is sweet, it's plain to see,
A jest among the foliage spree.
So let the ivy dance and play,
In rebel shades, they'll lead the way.

In the Shade of Growing Legends

In shadows thick where whispers roam,
Legends start with a funny gnome.
He wears a hat made of twigs and leaves,
Sipping tea from a cup that deceives.

His friends all gather on sunny days,
Telling tales in peculiar ways.
A squirrel joins with a dramatic flair,
As they plot schemes with giggles to spare.

A whimsical tale of who gets the nut,
With laughter echoing, they all strut.
Yet every time they plan a heist,
The nut rolls off like a highway twist!

In the shade of dreams where laughter grows,
Every legend deep down knows,
That fun is found in a jumbled rhyme,
Where silly stories stand the test of time.

Secrets of the Winding Path

Secrets hide where paths entwine,
Twisting tales like old grapevine.
A cat in shades with a poker face,
Makes bets on who will win the race.

A hedgehog deli serves snacky treats,
While frogs croak jokes; it's hard to beat.
The grass is ticklish, touch it if you dare,
You might just laugh till you lose your hair!

But watch your step, oh, heed the call,
Each corner might have a trickster ball.
With giggles hidden in the leaves,
The path reveals what your heart believes.

So stroll along, stay light on your feet,
The winding path is quite the feat.
In every turn and every sigh,
Is a tickle waiting to make you cry!

Linger in the Leafy Labyrinth

In a labyrinth where laughter grows,
Leaves chuckle softly, privacy flows.
A parrot perched on a leafy throne,
Tells tales of how he lost his bone.

Around each bend and twisty nook,
A pumpkin head tries to write a book.
It rolls away when it thinks you're near,
Chasing after 'til you squeal with cheer.

Mushrooms giggle, whispering loud,
While butterflies boast of fluffy clouds.
In this maze, silliness reigns supreme,
Where every corner hides a funny dream.

So linger here where frolic thrives,
In the leafy paths where laughter jives.
Each step unfolds a whimsical scheme,
A playful world beyond which we gleam.

The Riddle of the Climbing Soul

A climbing soul with a crooked grin,
Asks riddles that make the sun spin.
With vines that twist around his hat,
He giggles loud, 'What’s a cat in a spat?'

He climbs up high to reach the stars,
Telling jokes that’re simply bizarre.
'What's green and sings?’ you may implore,
'A rock star frog, oh, isn't he a bore?’

His friends, the birds, join in the jest,
Flapping wings, they never rest.
They swoop down low, and with each swoosh,
They brighten up a soggy moosh.

So if you see him scaling trees,
Join the laughter, be at ease.
For in every riddle, truth stands tall,
The climbing soul brings joy to all!

Interlacing Pathways

Through winding trails, the vines do giggle,
They tickle the toes, an unexpected wiggle.
With every turn, they twine and dance,
Offering nature a cheeky chance.

A leaf up high, whispers to a snail,
"Come on now, buddy, let’s tell a tale!"
The ants march on, oh, what a sight,
In this leafy maze, it’s pure delight.

A dandelion shouts, "I'm not just a weed!"
While petals sway, they plant a seed.
The hedgehog chuckles, as odd as it seems,
In these tangled paths, we all share dreams.

So grab a friend, let's take a spree,
In this botanical jamboree.
With laughter and vines intertwined,
Life’s little jokes are truly well-designed.

Shadows in the Sanctuary

Under the shade of a leafy crown,
A squirrel organizes a hoarding town.
"Fetch me an acorn!" he squeaks with glee,
While a crow cackles, "What a sight to see!"

A shadow on the grass does prance,
Turns out it’s just a squirrel’s mischance.
Ever so silent, the plants all stare,
As the rabbit tips over, unaware of despair.

Caterpillars giggle in synchronized rows,
Practicing lines for their next cabaret show.
Moths flutter by, already in style,
"Come join our dance, let's stay for a while!"

With whispers of leaves, the shadows play,
A decorum of silliness rules the day.
In this sanctuary where laughter's the key,
Nature’s quirks delight, as they should be.

The Elegy of Green Embrace

In a patch of moss, a frog’s on a spree,
Croaking ballads of mishap and glee.
A ladybug twirls, on her newfound throne,
Declare it a palace, in the green zones.

Beneath twisted branches, an artist does pout,
His canvas all messy, no doubt about.
With splashes of color, he muses aloud,
"I meant to paint beauty, but here's a loud crowd!"

A whippoorwill chuckles as shadows converge,
In this green embrace, a starlit surge.
The wind winks softly, through leaves it will hum,
"In nature's great chaos, we find a fun drum!"

So raise up a toast to the vines and the trees,
To mishaps and laughter, to nature’s decrees.
In this elegant mess, where beauty seems trite,
We dance with the green, into the night.

Poetics of a Vining Life

With tendrils curling, the stories unfold,
Of cheeky mischief, and secrets retold.
A berry below hums a jocular tune,
While a spider snickers, weaving under the moon.

The carrots discuss if they'll peek from the ground,
"Let’s join the bouquet, let’s dance all around!"
The onions, however, just keep to their cores,
Muttering softly, should we open these doors?

A wise old tree, with a laugh in his bark,
Says, “Life’s much funnier after dark!”
The fireflies twinkle, with giggles they glide,
In the vining life, we take each stride.

So gather the herbs for a cheerful feast,
Where laughter and greenery never cease.
As each leaf teases and bends to the rhyme,
We find joy in the growth as we savor our time.

Serenade of the Wandering Leaf

A leaf rolled by, it danced with glee,
It twirled and spun, so wild and free.
It met a bug, who wiggled near,
They laughed and joked, then shared a cheer.

On winding paths, they'd prance and play,
Creating mischief throughout the day.
The wind would sigh, a friendly tease,
As they would play just as they please.

Up high on branches, they'd weave a tale,
Of how they soared, though it was pale.
Yet all their dreams would rise and fall,
In laughter's grip, they had it all.

A leaf and bug, a duo bright,
In nature's realm, they found delight.
With every gust that sent them high,
They waved goodbye to clouds and sky.

Stories Caught in the Foliage

A squirrel sat with tales to share,
Of acorns lost and nuts laid bare.
He spoke of nights beneath the moon,
And how he danced to nature's tune.

The leaves would rustle, giggles rang,
With secrets whispered, laughter sang.
In tangled vines, the stories grew,
Of silly bumbles and friends anew.

A worm chimed in with squirming glee,
"Don't forget my slip from that tall tree!"
The crowd would roar, so full of cheer,
For every hiccup brought them near.

And when the sun began to fade,
The tales would twirl, but never jade.
In the embrace of every leaf,
Was joy and laughter, sweet relief.

In the Grasp of Verdant Dreams

In shades of green, a dream took flight,
Where plants would scheme by day and night.
A daisy said, “Let’s start a band!”
While vines began to take a stand.

They strummed on leaves and banged on bark,
Creating tunes from bright and dark.
With every note, the world would sway,
As petals burst in wild array.

A bee became their trusty coach,
“A concert here? Well, we’ll encroach!”
In every note, a cheer arose,
As nature danced in fragrant prose.

And when the moonlight took its turn,
The frolics started, hearts would churn.
With every laugh beneath the beams,
The plants would dream their verdant dreams.

Quandaries of a Climbing Heart

A vine fell in love with a garden wall,
It whispered sweetly, "I'll climb and sprawl!"
But oh, the struggles, the twist and turn,
To find the way, oh how it yearned.

It looped and wound, a dance so spry,
Yet faced dilemmas, oh my, oh my!
"Should I go right, or should I cling,
To every nod and bell that rings?"

With petals blushing, the daisies smiled,
As the vine got tangled, oh so riled.
Yet with each plight, a lesson learned,
In every failure, a passion burned.

At last, it found that love would grow,
Through every twist, it learned to flow.
So if you stumble, don't lose your spark,
For love is found in every arc.

Fables of a Living Wall

A wall once thought to be quite bare,
Found a friend in a vine with flair.
It climbed and hugged with all its might,
Turning dull gray into vibrant light.

The neighbors laughed, they thought it odd,
A plant that acted like a god.
'Upon my bricks, you can’t just live!'
Yet the vine’s dance was quite the gift.

One day it stretched, oh what a sight,
It tickled the roof, with pure delight.
The chimney smirked, the windows grinned,
As laughter spread through every wind.

So walls should host, that’s what they say,
A vine's wild charm can change the day.
With humor wrapped around each stone,
A living tale, not quite alone.

Between Stone and Softness

In a garden grown without a care,
A rock found love in a soft plant's hair.
They danced at dusk, two worlds collide,
A sturdy stone and a flowery guide.

The petals whispered jokes so sweet,
While the stone just stood—quite tough on its feet.
'Why don't you budge, oh solid friend?'
The plant chuckled, 'I can't pretend!'

Rainy days brought puddles near,
The stone just shrugged, 'I have no fear.'
'But I can float!' the flower cheered,
'While you stand firm, I've no need to be seared.'

With every downpour, the laughter grew,
A stone and a bloom, a comical crew.
Together they smiled, despite their strife,
Finding joy in their oddball life.

Harmony of the Wild Wanderer

A wanderer strolled with shoes all torn,
With leaves in their hair, they looked quite worn.
But every step was a jig and a dash,
As nature cheered and trees would clash.

The toadstools giggled, the birds took flight,
'This curious human seems quite all right!'
They twirled with vines, they pranced on grass,
Creating a scene that none could surpass.

Then came a breeze, a teasing gust,
As branches waved, in nature they thrust.
The wanderer twirled, lost in the song,
In a whimsical world where all felt wrong.

A tumble, a fall, and up they sprang,
With dirt on their nose, they laughed and sang.
For in the wild, a little absurd,
Life's a dance, not just a word.

Tales of the Twisting Bough

A bough that twists, so funny and free,
Swaying and bending as it drinks up the glee.
It whispered to leaves, 'Let’s put on a show!'
'We’ll entertain all, let's make spirits glow!'

The clouds chuckled down, sharing a grin,
As the bough did a jig, all ready to spin.
'No need for a stage, the woods are our place,'
They swayed to the rhythm, a leafy embrace.

Critters burst forth from their homes in delight,
A squirrel with a hat joined the dance that night.
A rabbit tried leaps, but fell in a pile,
Yet laughter erupted, quite silly in style.

With each little jolt and each wiggly way,
The bough kept them laughing, brightening the day.
So if you hear rustles, just join in the groove,
The bough knows the secret—how to dance and move!

Shadows in the Garden Light

In the garden where shadows dance,
A squirrel took a silly stance.
It flicked its tail, made a face,
Then tripped on air in a clumsy race.

The daisies giggled, the roses swayed,
As the sunbeam played a silly charade.
The worms below chuckled in their game,
While the flowers all whispered, "Who’s to blame?"

A bumblebee buzzed with a wobbly song,
But it bumped the daisies and spun along.
“Oh dear!” they cried with petals unfurled,
“What a comical buzz in our flower world!”

So under the light, with laughter so bright,
The garden became a comedic sight.
With shadows that giggled and blooms that cheered,
In this cozy corner, joy reappeared.

Tendrils of Memory

Tendrils twist where laughter grows,
Remembering silliness no one knows.
A cat on a fence made a daring leap,
And landed, oh so awkward, in a heap.

The ivy snickered, wrapped in green,
As the cat shook off, looking quite mean.
With a flick of the tail, it strutted away,
Unbothered by the hilarity of the day.

A ladybug, in dazzling red,
Rolled off a leaf, it's true, it said,
"I'm not clumsy, just practicing flair!"
And giggles erupted from everywhere.

So memories linger where laughter resounds,
In tendrils of joy that forever surrounds.
With each twist and turn, every giggle and cheer,
The past mixes fondly with a light-hearted tear.

The Quiet Embrace of Leaves

Leaves whisper secrets in softest tones,
While squirrels play fetch with acorn stones.
A rustle reveals a wily grey thief,
Who, quite flustered, forgot his motif.

In the quiet, a rabbit giggles away,
Wobbling at shadows, attempting to play.
The leaves chuckle at the movie they're in,
As the sun peeks through, with a wide, goofy grin.

A butterfly flutters, thinking it sly,
But lands on a frog, who lets out a sigh.
"Oh pardon me, I'm just here for the show!"
And the leaves tossed laughter, letting it flow.

Beneath the canopy, where chuckles convene,
Life is a comedy, frantically serene.
Amidst all the laughter, sweet moments entwine,
In the quiet embrace, so perfectly fine.

Beneath the Climbing Embrace

Beneath vines that twist and climb,
A family of frogs had quite the time.
They practiced their leaps with giggles galore,
Each one landing with a surprising roar!

The older ones croaked, "We'll show you the way!"
While the younger ones hopped, come what may.
With tumbles and splashes, they made such a mess,
But oh! All the laughter, who could second guess?

A wandering snail watched, shaking its head,
"Why leap through the air when you could crawl instead?"

But the frogs just laughed and leaped even higher,
Creating a show that could never expire.

So beneath the embrace, where nonsense prevails,
The giggles and joy create happy trails.
With each bound and leap, and each chuckling cheer,
Life is a frolic, so joyful, so dear!

The Wall's Gentle Confessions

Whispers of plaster, secrets spill,
Laughter in shadows, a lighthearted thrill.
Climbing with gusto, green fingers play,
Wall's gentle confessions, a funny ballet.

Colors of mischief, where stories blend,
Leaves giggle softly, to vines they tend.
A dance of the daring, with roots all askew,
Wall wears a crown of a wild leafy crew.

Echoes of chuckles from bricks worn and cold,
Each tendril a tale, a mystery told.
Embracing the space, with humor and glee,
The wall chuckles back, as green guests agree.

With vibrant ambitions, they reach for the skies,
In a whimsical race, they all try to rise.
As laughter ascends in the creeping parade,
The wall's gentle confessions, a verdant charade.

A Symphony in Green

In the heart of a garden, a cacophony thrives,
Bugs join the chorus, as humor arrives.
The leaves drop a wink, the petals all hum,
Nature’s own band played on, oh what fun!

Bouncing and jiving, the breeze takes its cue,
Each branch plays a note, as the rhythm breaks through.
A polka of petals, a waltz of the weeds,
Witty exchanges lead to giggly deeds.

A serenade written in chlorophyll flows,
With melodies echoing, as each laughter grows.
The compost is clapping, the flowers all sway,
Nature’s symphony, in laughter they play.

So come take a listen, let nature expose,
The funny symphony that the green garden chose.
With roots drumming beats, and vines all in tune,
Underneath sun's smile, life orchestrates noon.

Secrets Woven in the Leaves

Secrets are tangled, in the tendrils they hide,
A mischief of petals, where laughter resides.
Leaves giggle softly, with whispers they share,
A tapestry woven, of fun everywhere.

The breeze takes a selfie with branches on show,
Snap! There's a chuckle, in each leafy row.
What tales do they tell, under moon's gentle beams?
A dance of the quirky, in whimsical dreams.

Do you see that gnome, peeking just so?
He's cracking up nightly, with secrets to grow.
The flowers all snicker, as night time descends,
In this leafy playground, where humor transcends.

So next time you wander, take a good look,
At secrets entwined in the great green book.
For nature's own laughter, is liberally found,
In the whispers of leaves, and joy all around.

Under a Canopy of Time

A canopy’s giggle, where shadows do sway,
Tickling the silence, in a playful ballet.
Time takes a breather, beneath leafy cheer,
Whispers of laughter ring crystal and clear.

Branches stretch out, like arms open wide,
They beckon the sunbeams to join in the ride.
When moments play tag, and memories chase,
A merry-go-round, in nature's embrace.

As clouds pass above, like cotton candy fluff,
They join in the fun, though it’s never quite tough.
A tickle of wind, a humorous muse,
Time dances lightly, in laughter’s sweet shoes.

So laugh with the leaves, as they wiggle and sway,
Under a canopy where joy leads the way.
Moments collide, like confetti of cheer,
In this timeless adventure, forever appears.

Whispers in the Shade

In the garden, plants conspire,
Laughter blooms, they never tire.
A gnome grins, caught in a spree,
Talking gossip 'neath the tree.

Beneath the leaves, secrets flop,
A bug dances, ‘Hey! Don't stop!’
Bees buzz jokes, a merry hum,
Nature’s jesters, never glum.

Dandelions push for a joke,
While willow branches sway and poke.
With every rustle, a chuckle bursts,
In this world, humor never thirsts.

So come and join this leafy play,
Where laughter sprinkles every day.
In the shade, where fun runs wild,
Even nature can be quite the child.

Embraced by Nature’s Touch

In the glen, the bushes grin,
Tickled by wind, they spin and spin.
A squirrel plots a daring heist,
As acorns roll; oh what a feast!

Flowers flutter, dressed in cheer,
They wink at shoes that wander near.
A butterfly steals the show,
In a dance, it twirls just so.

Grass blades whisper, “Come and play!”
Even thorns are fun today.
Roots giggle under soil's cover,
While crickets sing for one another.

Watch the vines wrap all around,
Nature’s fun can surely astound.
In this embrace, smiles abound,
Laughter in every leaf is found.

The Climbing Chronicles

Up the wall, the green stuff creeps,
A secret path where mischief leaps.
It tickles bricks with leafy hands,
Plotting pranks in the flower lands.

A raccoon peeks from a leafy throne,
Shouting, “Hey! You’re too late, I’ve grown!”
With each twist, and every turn,
These climbs of laughter make hearts burn.

The ivy whispers tales so bold,
Of sneaky spiders and webs of gold.
A snail slides down, what a sight!
“I’m late for class! You’re all so bright!”

Watch the tendrils reach for fun,
Boundless joy beneath the sun.
In this tale of climbs unmatched,
Laughter’s roots are firmly latched.

Beneath Nature's Tangle

Amidst the chaos, joy unfolds,
As curious vines do as they're told.
With jests and jives, they intertwine,
Spinning tales on a playful line.

The hedgehogs giggle, rolled in leaves,
While toads wear crowns, nothing deceives.
Nature's wild, a crazy kin,
Where every knot holds laughter in.

Twisted branches arch with glee,
As chipmunks chase a bumblebee.
In tangled roots of joy, they slip,
All secrets shared in nature's grip.

So join the frolic, don't delay,
In this madness where we sway.
Beneath the weave of green's delight,
Silly moments take to flight.

The Sound of Green Stories

In the garden, whispers play,
Breezes tease the vines each day.
Laughter bounces off the leaves,
Nature's antics, oh, it cleaves!

A squirrel dons a leafy hat,
He struts around, oh, such a brat!
Robins chuckle, gossips flow,
In this realm, the giggles grow.

The vines gossip under the sun,
Sharing secrets, oh, such fun!
Each tendril tells a silly tale,
Of garden pranks that never fail.

Amidst the green, a frog will croak,
In perfect pitch, he plays a joke.
Nature's chorus, wild and free,
Celebrates the joy we see.

Emblems of the Untamed

A dandelion wishes to fly,
It dreams of heights beyond the sky.
Yet stuck in soil, it seems so bold,
Cracking jokes as it grows old.

A snail wearing a shell for a hat,
Calls itself the fastest of that!
Tickled leaves, they laugh and sway,
At the slowpoke creeping away.

A raccoon with a cupcake grin,
Steals the shine, oh, where to begin?
The grapes roll eyes from the vine,
"It's a heist!" they snicker in line.

In playful chaos, critters dance,
Twisting branches in a trance.
In this jungle, laughter reigns,
The untamed giggles run through the veins.

Portrait of the Hanging Green

Watch as creepers unfold bright,
Decorating trunks, what a sight.
A wise old oak wears leafy shades,
Pretending wisdom never fades.

The rain drops like a drummer's beat,
Pitter-patter, it’s a treat!
Flowers sway and toss their heads,
As bees play tag on floral beds.

A lizard sunbathes, so carefree,
Strikes a pose, just wait and see!
With a wink, it steals the show,
The leafy crowd gasps, “Whoa, whoa!”

In this portrait of green so grand,
The antics never go as planned.
Each vine giggles, each petal sighs,
In a world where humor flies.

Through the Leafy Veil

A curtain of green where secrets dwell,
Behind the leaves, stories swell.
With a rustle, a raccoon peeks,
Wonders of mischief, its eyes speak.

In the underbrush, a dance unfolds,
Little feet chase, while the world scolds.
A worm in a hat, a sight to see,
“Dress code’s fancy!” it claims with glee.

Around the bend, a shadow looms,
Blossoms shriek as laughter blooms.
“Oh dear, it’s a party crash!”
A hedgehog whirls, a quick panache!

Through the leafy veil we see,
A jester’s reign, pure jubilee!
With every rustle, every twist,
In green’s embrace, we can’t resist.

www.ingramcontent.com/pod-product-compliance
Ingram Content Group UK Ltd.
Pitfield, Milton Keynes, MK11 3LW, UK
UKHW021635160125
4140UKWH00033B/427

9 781805 668640